Text
Bill Harris

CLB 2775
© 1991 Colour Library Books Ltd, Godalming, Surrey, England.
All rights reserved.
This 1991 edition published by Crescent Books,
distributed by Outlet Book Company, Inc, a Random House Compan
225 Park Avenue South, New York, New York 10003.
Printed in Hong Kong.
ISBN 0 517 06041 8
8 7 6 5 4 3 2 1

HAWAII
FROM THE AIR

CRESCENT BOOKS
NEW YORK

The mossy folds of the Pali Coast, Molokai.

"Paradise" is a word that's used more often than any other to describe the Hawaiian Islands. That's because no other word fits quite so well. It's not uncommon to hear tourists remark that if Heaven isn't like this, they don't want to go there. And tourists are going to Hawaii in waves as spectacular as the ocean waves that break on those fabulous beaches. About three million visitors arrive in Hawaii every year, mostly from the United States. But of the million-plus Japanese tourists who visit the United States every year, 75 percent go to Hawaii. Japanese-Americans rank second in numbers behind "Haole," the name native Hawaiians use for mainland whites, so visitors from Japan feel right at home. Just as important, probably, is the fact that Honolulu is just six jet hours from Tokyo.

The jet plane is what is behind the Hawaiian tourist boom. Back in the 1950s, when Hawaii became a state, most Americans who went there were from California, and most of them went by boat. It was a leisurely, unforgettable experience for them. One man, who made the trip several times, describes it this way:

"On the fourth morning out from San Francisco, you'd wake up to see Molokai there on the left and Oahu on the right. Rounding Diamond Head, the biggest thing on the island looked to be a pink, Moorish palace, the Royal Hawaiian Hotel.

"The ship would take on three tugloads of greeters, and move on to the dock at Aloha Tower, where the Royal Hawaiian Band and hula girls met you."

The weekly arrival of the big white ship *Lurline* from San Francisco was called "Steamer Day" in the Honolulu of the 1950s. The mainlanders, who had invested five days to get there, got a welcome that was unrivalled anywhere in the world. The air was perfumed with the heavy scent of tropical flowers, the green mountains accentuated the dramatic cliffs, and the beautiful white beaches presented a picture that could only conjure up that same word again, "paradise."

And, to add pleasure to the paradise, the mainlanders were met by those beautiful hula girls singing the love songs of their Polynesian ancestors, while in the water below the slow-moving ship, native divers raced to the bottom of the crystal clear harbor to retrieve silver dollars tossed overboard by the visitors.

People who go to Hawaii today get there faster and spend less time getting acclimated when they do. But the legendary hospitality that is Hawaii and the spectacular beauty make their first impression of the place just as memorable today as it ever was.

The Islands, flung like a strand of pearls into the middle of the Pacific Ocean, are about 2,500 miles from San Francisco. There are about 132 islands in all, some not inhabited at all, some private preserves of single families. In total area, Hawaii is two-thirds the size of Sicily, but bigger than Massachusetts. The eight major islands in the Southeast: Hawaii, Oahu, Maui, Kahoolawe, Kauai, Molokai and Niihau, make up all but three square miles of the total area.

Honolulu and Pearl Harbor are on the island of Oahu, which is where some 80 percent of the state's population lives. The biggest island, Hawaii, is also the farthest south – in fact, the tip of Volcanoes National Park forms the southernmost point of the United States.

It's always spring in Hawaii because of the cooling winds from the Pacific, which keep the year round temperatures in the neighborhood of 75°F. And the sun shines just about all the time. The Islanders thank one of their gods, Maui, for that. They say that many years ago he hid in the forest until the sun came out. When it did, he lassoed it and tied it down so it couldn't move. The sun didn't like that very much, according to the legend, but Maui wouldn't let it go until it promised to move more slowly across his islands. A promise given is a promise kept when you're the sun. And the promise is still being kept all these centuries later.

Honolulu is the capital city and its population reflects the mixture of people you'll find on all the islands. Less than half are Haoles, Western whites; about a quarter are Japanese and about 15 percent are descended from the original Polynesians who were the first to arrive there. The balance of the population is Filipino, Chinese, Korean, and others.

It's an exotic blend that's sheer joy for people-watchers. The delicate features of the Japanese, the handsome faces of the Chinese, the legendary beauty of the Polynesians add up to a spectacle that's hard to resist. Even the Haole seem more beautiful here than anywhere else.

Downtown Honolulu today doesn't look much different from Houston or any other American city that has gone through a building boom in the last twenty years. But don't let that fool you. There is a difference! Sure, Kalakaua Avenue, like main streets in other parts of the country, has been converted to a car-less shopping mall, the convention halls and continental restaurants are air-conditioned, and you stand a good chance of meeting someone from your home town when you go there on a vacation – but you begin to notice the difference when you sit on a terrace overlooking the Pacific and are served local pineapple or papaya for breakfast. You see it in the side streets, or in a Chinese cemetery, where families feed their dead to keep them contented. You hear it in the streets where the old Hawaiian songs still haunt the air. You get a sense of the past in Honolulu's Bishop

Museum, founded as a memorial to a Hawaiian princess who married a New Englander aged 18.

Mrs. Bishop was heiress to the lands and treasures of the Kamehameha family, and those treasures form the nucleus of the museum's collection. The old royal thrones and crown are found here, along with a rare collection of feathered adornments made for the chiefs and kings of old Hawaii. The rich colors and design of the cloaks impressed Captain Cook, who noted in his journal that: "…even in countries where dress is more attended to, [they] might be reckoned elegant. The ground of them is a net-work upon which the most beautiful red and yellow feathers are so closely fixed that the surface might be compared to the thickest and richest velvet."

The Bishop Museum also has a planetarium, reflecting an interest in the stars that goes back to the earliest times. Today, one of the world's most important astronomical observatories is on the Island of Hawaii, at the top of Mount Mauna Kea. The summit of the volcano is almost 14,000 feet high, so high that clouds rarely pass over it, and astronomers feel it's the best place in the Northern Hemisphere for looking out into the universe.

The Island of Oahu, where Honolulu is located, is relatively small, and can be explored easily. It's ringed by beaches, the most famous of which is Waikiki. The Hawaiian royal family reserved Waikiki for themselves, but the Hawaiians of today have turned it over to the tourists – they go to Ala Moana Beach, not far away, for swimming and tanning. When it's surfing they want, they load their surfboards on their cars and head north to Makaha or another of the "big surf" beaches across the island. For snorkeling, they go to the underwater sanctuary at Hanauma Bay. For privacy they journey past the "Blowhole" – a dramatic geyser that erupts every time the waves hit a hole in the lava ledge, sending a a huge waterspout into the air – to get to Halona Cove, a small beach hidden away between the cliffs.

Diamond Head, an extinct volcano, is also on the Island of Oahu. You can climb inside the crater and have a look around, if you like. The old Hawaiians called it Leahi, which means "the place of fire." It got a new name from British sailors who thought they had found diamonds there. What they really found were volcanic crystals.

Visitors to Oahu can get a glimpse of Samoa and Tahiti, New Zealand or Fiji, by visiting the Polynesian Cultural Center. It consists of a collection of villages of the kind that would be found on other islands with a Polynesian tradition. Young Polynesians work their way through college by demonstrating the old ways of life, singing and dancing in authentic native costume. Old Hawaii can also be glimpsed at there, in a village of triangular houses covered in pili grass … the famous "little grass shacks" you often hear about but don't see much in Hawaii these days.

There's a bird sanctuary on Oahu too, called Paradise Park (there's that word again!). There are also 15 golf courses, 90 tennis courts, 50 miles of beaches and 600 places to go surfing on this island. And just so you don't get homesick, there is Ala Moana Shopping Center, one of the biggest in the world. Most of the hotels have their own shopping malls, too. In fact, about the only thing that makes the hotels of Oahu different from those you'd find in any American city with palm trees and a beach is that they all offer church services every Sunday morning in their schedule of activities – just one more way the influence of the missionaries hangs on.

Pearl Harbor, named for the pearl oysters that once thrived there, is part of the Oahu scene. The Hawaiians believed this was originally the home of Kaahupahua, the queen of the sharks. She lived, they said, in a cavern that was a majestic palace guarded by a brother shark. She protected the people by decreeing that sharks should not molest humans, and she backed her decree with an order to her shark people to be constantly on the alert to kill any man-eaters that might invade the waters near the island.

Jumbo jets deliver tourists, hundreds at a time, to Honolulu airport. If they're from New York, they've been on the plane for 13 hours and they've had to push their watches ahead another six hours. But, if they prefer to be on the real Hawaiian time, they take their watches off. Radio and television stations are about the only institutions in the Islands that follow anything like a strict time schedule, and even they occasionally forget. There's a carillon in Waikiki that plays Hawaiian tunes as it strikes the hour, but the

music rarely begins until the hour is at least 10 minutes old.

Most of the mainlanders and others who pass through the airport stay right on Oahu, but there is great enthusiasm building for the other islands. Many visitors hop onto a hydrofoil to go 22 miles east to Molokai, the one they call "the friendly isle." Still a little off the beaten path, it manages to retain some of the character of the old Hawaii.

There are huge pineapple plantations on Molokai, and cattle ranches too. King Kamehameha V himself raised longhorns out here in the 1860s. When he wasn't "rasslin' steers," he found time to plant a grove of 1,000 coconut trees on ten acres just outside Kaunakaki, the island's main town.

Just beyond Molokai is Lanai, the "Pineapple Island." It's owned by Castle & Cook, a company most people may know of   because it owns the Dole Company. They bought the island, 18 by 13 miles wide, back in 1922 for $1,100,000. They built a company town there and transformed the island into a huge pineapple plantation with good roads and a deep-water port.

Lanai is also a paradise for hunters. It abounds in pronghorn antelope, partridge, pheasant and wild goats. In some parts of the island the season is open all the year for bow and arrow hunting.

For years, the "in" crowd, film stars and the like, have been going to the island of Maui, which is quite different from all the others. It was created by two big volcanoes which formed two mountain masses joined together by a thin strip of land. The strip of land is where you'll find most of the hotels and condominiums that make this the second most popular tourist island in Hawaii. One of the things they go there to see is Haleakala, the largest dormant volcano in the world – it's worth the trip! The mountain is more than 10,000 feet high and the crater is 21 miles around. Inside it lie caverns, a lake, meadows, forests, even a desert, and the biggest raspberry bushes you will probably ever see.

The natives call Kauai the "garden island," but its landscape includes some awesome cliffs and rugged canyons as well as brightly colored flowers and lush trees that spill over into the water at the edge of smooth, sandy beaches. The beaches are nearly deserted most of the time, and inland you could spend hours wandering through quiet valleys and not see another soul.

Photographers can't get enough of Kauai. Waimea Canyon is a place they adore because the look of the place changes from hour to hour as the light changes. The Wailua River, once considered so sacred it didn't have a name lest someone would be tempted to talk about it, is the setting for several ancient temples. One of them was called a "temple of refuge," placed there as a sanctuary where someone who had broken a tabu or had been defeated in battle could be guaranteed safety. But there was a catch: the transgressor had to get there ahead of the people who were chasing him.

One of Hawaii's most fascinating resort hotels, Coco Palms, is on Kauai. It was built to conform to the old traditions and to recreate as many of them as possible. Every evening at dusk, a group of young men sound a note on conch shells, first in the direction of the mountains, then towards the sea. It's an ancient signal to everyone within earshot that "the drums will talk." As they finish, the drums do talk in a beat that announces that a feast has been prepared. And that, in turn, signals the lighting of torches in the hotel's 30-acre palm grove.

There's a spectacular waterspout on this island too. When the surf hits a hole in the rock called "Spouting Horn," it sends a jet of water 100 feet into the air. And when that happens you can hear what sounds like a deep sigh from another hole nearby. It's the sound, the natives say, of a dragon who swam in there centuries ago and can't find his way out.

Less than 20 miles away, but hundreds of years distant, is the tiny island of Niihau. According to legend, no one may ever visit there, and if a Hawaiian leaves, he or she is forbidden to return. That's not quite true today. Visitors are allowed to go to Niihau, but only as invited guests. And Hawaiians who leave are welcomed back.

A century ago, Elizabeth Sinclair, a Scottish woman from New Zealand, having lost her husband, packed all her belongings and her children and grandchildren into a small boat and set out for Canada. She stopped off in Honolulu where she met King Kamehameha IV. He was so charmed by her that he offered to give her some land nearby. She had cattle ranching on her mind and so refused the offer and sailed on. She went to Vancouver, but not liking what she found there, she loaded up the schooner again and went back to Hawaii.

She paid the king £10,000 for the 72-square mile island of Niihau, and got some coastal land on Kauai in the bargain. Her son-in-law, a man named Robinson, became the lord of the island, and when he died about 35 years ago, his widow and five children became the sole owners of Niihau. There are 300 people living there now, all pure-blooded Hawaiians, all speaking the unchanged language of their forefathers.

In spite of the intrusion of TV sets, newspapers and other trappings of the 20th century, Niihau is one of the last places on earth where simple feudal life still exists, and it's the only place where old Hawaii is little changed.

The word Hawaii conjures up an image of gentle breezes and bright sunshine, and that's why people go there. But a lot of people go there to watch the sun set because it probably doesn't go down as beautifully anywhere in the world as it does off the Kona Coast on the big island that gave all the islands it name: Hawaii. The huge volcano Mauna Loa keeps the wind away from the coast, and every morning it's bright and sunny there because the clouds can't get over the mountain. They often win the battle by the middle of the day, and when they do they act like an umbrella that keeps the hot sun off the beach and the temperature down. Combined with the rich soil of the volcano, it makes a perfect atmosphere for growing coffee, and plenty of it's grown there. In fact, Hawaii is the only place in the United States where you'll find coffee plantations. One of the biggest cattle ranches in the United States is right near the Kona Coast. The Parker Ranch has been growing ever since a New Englander, John Palmer Parker, gave up the life of a sailor to become a cowboy in 1847. His spread was no threat to the big guys who were getting themselves established in the American Southwest at the time. It was only two acres. It's grown today to well over a quarter of a million acres. And it has the big advantage over its Texas competitors of that wonderful Hawaiian seacoast. And those sunsets!

Most of the beaches on the islands are made of fine white sand that feels terrific underfoot. It feels so good, in fact, that the missionaries, persuasive as they were, were never able to talk the Hawaiian people into wearing shoes. Even today, the islands aren't exactly a paradise for shoe salesmen. On the big island, Hawaii, the fine white sand comes in a variety of colors, including green at one point. But the most unusual is to be found on the southern coast, where the beaches and sand dunes are black.

This coast is the traditional home of the fire goddess, Pele, and the black sand is just one example of her work. Another is the island itself, which is more than twice as big as all the other islands put together. And it's getting bigger because Pele is still at it. She breathes fire through the huge Mauna Loa volcano, and sometimes, when the mood strikes her, she make Kilauea boil over. The territory around the mountains, now a national park, is an experience no one ever forgets. The black beaches and sand dunes, made of pulverized lava, are just the beginning. Going into Hawaii Volcanoes National Park is like going into another world. Thousands of acres are covered with cinders and a hard crust of lava that has solidified into patterns and looks like a neglected pan of molasses. There's a whole forest of the ghosts of trees whose roots were sealed off by a lava flow; and another living forest that was left undisturbed when a lava river forked around a 100 space for form a green island in the midst of the desolation. There's a hotel and a golf course in the park, in probably the most unusual setting for either thing anywhere in the world.

But what makes the park truly unique is Mauna Loa and Kilauea, both very much alive. It's possible to get to the top of Mauna Loa and look into its awesome fire pit. There's a paved road about halfway up the side of the mountain, but after that, it's an 18-mile hike to the summit. Hardy hikers say the trip is worth the effort, but most people prefer to take their word for it.

Kilauea has the advantage of being easier to climb. The trip to the top is 9,000 feet shorter and, with a little bit of luck, people who take the trip see volcanic activity inside the crater, even an occasional eruption. Every once in a while, somebody reports seeing Pele herself. She's beautiful and still young, they say, with long flowing red hair. Sometimes she even talks to them to explain where the next river of fiery lava will go. When that happens, there's no guarantee it will actually happen that way, though. Pele has been known to change her mind.

Most people drive around the rim in their cars. There is an observation platform on the brink of it, giving an unforgettable view of the fire pit inside. The pit is like a big kettle about a half-mile around and about 750 feet deep. That's where the spectacular fire fountains and melted lava come from. Most of the time, the lava stays inside the crater, but now and then, Pele decides to put on a show and the whole thing spills over. When it does, the island grows a little more.

Every now and then, nature takes a little away from the big island. Huge tidal waves which the natives call *tsunamis*, have come roaring across the Pacific, even in recent times, to bring havoc to the island's main city, Hilo. Every time one has hit, Hilo has hit back, moving a little bit farther inland and putting up bigger and better breakwaters against the next tsunami.

They're a tough bunch, these Hawaiians. Nothing keeps them down for long. They have endured volcanic eruptions, tidal waves, tourist invasions, even missionaries, with good-humored charm. They'll jump at any excuse for a good party, and the best party in any of the 50 states is an authentic Hawaiian luau.

Today luaus are staple fare at most of the big hotels, and you'll find everybody from the Lauloowoona chapter of Hadassah to the friendly sons of Polynesia sponsoring them for profit as well as for fun. In the beginning, the luau was the big event in small villages, in a tradition similar to that of New England's clambakes. The name itself means "taro leaf," which the old-timers used for food. Their parties were held in the center of the villages, and everybody in town was invited … indeed, everybody in town helped prepare it. Lit by festive torches, the setting incorporates the dazzling flowers and tropical foliage that create so much of the charm of the islands.

It took the whole day to get a good luau together. First the men dug a huge pit and lined it with rocks. Then they built a fire to heat the rocks. Next, they split a pig open, filled it with heated rocks and wrapped it in taro leaves. The pig was buried in the pit and left to roast most of the day. By the time it was ready to eat, it was the best-tasting roast pig any culture ever devised.

But man cannot live by pork alone. Not at a luau. The bill of fare also included roast chicken, laulau – a piece of pork wrapped together with salmon and roasted – baked yams with pineapple, shredded salmon mixed with fresh tomatoes and onions and eaten raw, and steamed taro leaves. Poi was also on the menu, served with dried seaweed. And for dessert there was coconut cream pudding, called noupio.

If anyone implies that eating native food in Hawaii is bad for your health, don't believe it! Hawaiians are the healthiest people in the United States. Life expectancy in the U.S. is just under 73 years at this point. The average Hawaiian can expect to live almost 76 years, and Hawaiian women average almost 78 years.

Hawaiian women almost never die in childbirth. Heart disease, cancer and strokes kill far fewer in Hawaii than anywhere else in the country. Of course, with that climate, they don't get pneumonia or 'flu very often, either. And to top it all off, the ratio of doctors to the population is among America's highest.

It isn't clear whether the "Aloha Spirit" keeps them alive or whether they stay around longer to enjoy the "Aloha Spirit." But that spirit is something that makes Hawaii unique among the 50 states.

It's a combination of remembering history and respecting tradition. It's taking joy from beauty and honoring grace. It's taking paradise seriously.

Hawaiians do all those things. Their life is generally joyful, and joy is like a contagious disease – as anyone who has ever been close to it knows very well.

The Pali Coast on the island of Molokai is one of the most spectacular coastlines in the Islands.

Above: a beautiful golden beach and resort development on Kauai, the Garden Isle, where sugar cane fields (top and left) cover the hills and reach to shores lapped by the Pacific Ocean.

15

Above, top and overleaf right: the pleated cliffs of Na Pali Coast, Kauai (these pages and overleaf), rising up to 3,000 feet above the crashing surf and deep, jungled valleys. Right and overleaf left: the walls of Waimea Canyon, in Waimea Canyon State Park, tower over 2,000 feet above Waimea River.

Above and top: Koloa Coast, Kauai (these pages and overleaf).
Right: Makahuena Point. Overleaf: (left) the lush vegetation of
Waimea Canyon, and (right) farm crops in the central plantations,
by Waimea Canyon.

Below, left and overleaf right: Hanauma Bay and Koko Head, Oahu (these pages and overleaf). Bottom: Makapuu Point, famous for body-surfing competitions. Overleaf left: Koko Crater, rising to 1,208 feet, provides magnificent scenic views.

Waikiki (above and overleaf left), a peninsula about half a mile wide by two miles long, is now a major tourist attraction. Top, right and overleaf right: Diamond Head, Oahu (these pages and overleaf). The crater was formed 150,000 years ago by a series of underwater volcanic explosions.

These pages: Waikiki, Oahu, its skyscrapers overlooking Waikiki Beach – a series of golden, sandy beaches lapped by the gentle waters of the Pacific. Left: the Ala Wai Yacht Harbor, at the mouth of Ala Wai Canal, sheltering more than 1,000 private boats.

Right: Ala Wai Yacht Harbor, Waikiki Beach (these pages), Oahu.

Left: the Waimea Mountains, seen from Haleiwa, on the north coast of Oahu (these pages). Below: Waimea Falls Park, and (bottom) Waimea Bay.

These pages: the Kona Coast at Kailua, Oahu. Here, Hawaii's tropical waters provide a good site for snorkelers and deep-sea fishing.

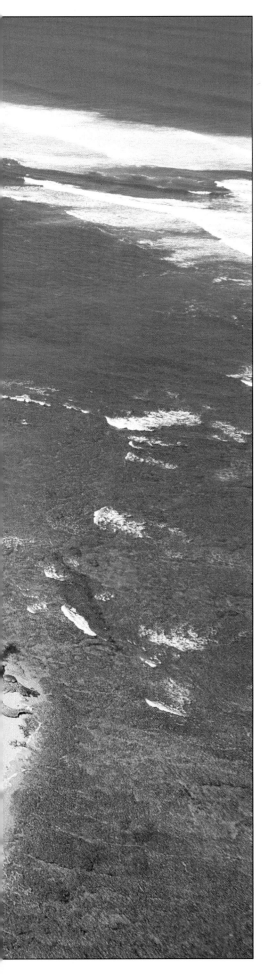

The coast from Kawela to Waimea Bay offers magnificent winter surfing, some waves reaching as high as thirty feet. Above: Kahuku, seen from Kahuku Point. Left: Kawela Bay. Top: Turtle Bay and the Kuilima Hyatt Hotel. Overleaf: the Koolau Mountains, Oahu (these pages).

41

Below: Mahie Point, Oahu (these pages). Left: Laniloa Point.
Bottom: Laie, a settlement of Hawaiian and Polynesian Mormons.

Below: the Moke Lua Islands, sanctuaries for seabirds. Moke O Loe, or the Coconut Island (bottom), off Oahu (these pages), was once a private estate, but is now part of the University of Hawaii's marine biology department. Right: the view over Nuupia Ponds and Kaneohe Bay to Kalaeoio Point.

The lush green vegetation of Oahu Island rolls over the Waianae Mountains (above), Makaha Point (top) and Makua Valley (right).

Below: Honolulu, seen from the Koolau Mountains of Oahu (these pages and overleaf). Bottom: Maili Point. The U.S.S *Arizona* Memorial (left) spans the hulk in which 1,102 men died when the Japanese bombed Pearl Harbor in 1941. Overleaf: (left) Honolulu, and (right) the National Memorial Cemetery.

Above and top: the Pali Coast, Molokai. Here, waterfalls tumble thousands of feet to the ocean below and caves cut into the heart of the island. Right: the dramatic cliffs of Maui. Overleaf: (left) orderly farmland in the valleys of Keanae, on Maui, and (right) ranches spread across Molokai.

Below: the cliffs of Pali, Molokai. Right: patchwork fields of Keanae on Maui Island. Bottom and overleaf right: sugar plantations in the central valley of Maui. Overleaf left: Lahaina, an historic Maui waterfront town which became a focal point of the whaling industry during the nineteenth century.

The graceful cliffs of the Hamakua Coast (these pages and overleaf left) line the northeast shore of Hawaii; lush green vegetation clings to the vertical cliffs, and waterfalls appear from the jungled slopes and cascade down into the Pacific Ocean. Overleaf right: Hona Kane Valley.

The magical combination of blue sea, sandy beaches, volcanic sculpturing and hot weather make Hawaii (these pages) and the Hawaiian islands irresistible to vacationers. Even though over three million tourists visit the islands every year, very few of the beaches ever become crowded.

These pages and overleaf: Mauna Lani Bay Hotel, adjacent to the crescent-shaped beach of Makaiwa Bay, Hawaii.

Mauna Lani Bay Hotel's man-made greens (these pages) combine with the lava obstacles to create one of the most challenging golf courses in the state.

Parker Ranch (below), Hawaii (these pages and overleaf). Right and bottom: ranchland on the Hamakua Coast.

INDEX

Mauna Kea State Park. Atop its 13,796-foot-high volcano stands
Mauna Kea Observatory.